This page left intentionally blank.

Message from the Program Director

One of the Department of Homeland Security's (DHS) priorities is the protection of Federal employees and private citizens who work within and visit United State government-owned or -leased facilities. The Interagency Security Committee (ISC), established by Executive Order 12977 and chaired by DHS, consists of 60 Federal departments and agencies and has as its mission the development of security standards and best practices for non-military Federal facilities in the United States.

As Program Director of the ISC, I am pleased to introduce the new ISC document titled *Federal Mobile Workplace Security: An Interagency Security Committee White Paper*. This ISC white paper provides a set of recommendations for action that will shape policy and standardize procedures that agencies housed in non-military Federal facilities can use to ensure the security of telework arrangements and alternative workspaces and the employees who utilize them. This document also defines key terms to identify policy and planning considerations, expected behaviors, and approaches for agencies to implement mobile work solutions in the Federal workplace to ensure the security of employees, their workplace, sensitive/unclassified information, and the public.

This white paper is a significant milestone and represents exemplary collaboration across the ISC and among the ISC Future of Federal Workplace Security Working Group. With full concurrence, ISC Primary Members approved this white paper will review and update the document as needed.

Daryle Hernandez
Program Director
Interagency Security Committee

Table of Contents

1.0   Background

The Interagency Security Committee (ISC) was formed by Executive Order (E.O.) 12977 signed by President Bill Clinton in 1995 following the Oklahoma City bombing. This devastating event prompted the White House to establish a permanent body to address the continuing government-wide physical security needs for Federal facilities. Today, the ISC is chaired by the Department of Homeland Security (DHS) and consists of a permanent body with representatives from 60 Federal agencies and departments.

Since the inception of the ISC, developments in technology introduced a virtual or cyber component to the Federal facilities security profile. Like the physical security element for the Federal worker environment, the virtual or cybersecurity element also requires analysis and review.

On December 9, 2010, President Barack Obama signed the Telework Enhancement Act of 2010.[1] The Telework Enhancement Act broadens the traditional Federal facility to include employee duties and responsibilities at approved worksites other than the normal employee workplace.

In response to the implementation of the Telework Enhancement Act as well as to other new policy directives, the ISC created the Future of Federal Workplace Security Working Group to assess the impact on physical and cybersecurity policies and practices. The working group was chartered to:

- Survey existing requirements, guidance, and pilot programs regarding telework and alternative workplaces and associated security;

- Analyze current requirements for information technology (IT) security and physical security and make recommendations on how those activities should overlap or be integrated;

- Recommend appropriate roles and responsibilities for employees, supervisors, and security providers regarding telework and alternative workplace security, including responsibility and requirements for staffing and training; and

- Recommend common standards and processes that should be developed to ensure telework and alternative workplace security.

Based on the working group's findings, the ISC presents the Federal security community *Federal Mobile Workplace Security: An ISC White Paper*.

---

[1] Public Law 111-292; 5 USC § 6501 - 06: Telework Enhancement Act of 2010.

2.0 Applicability and Scope

The *Federal Mobile Workplace Security White Paper* is a reference for Federal agencies when implementing mobile Federal workplace security. This document defines key terms, identifies existing policy and security planning considerations, and outlines expected behaviors to include methods for agencies to utilize when implementing mobile Federal workplace solutions.

On February 12, 2013, two key documents were released by the White House: the Presidential Policy Directive 21 (PPD-21), *Critical Infrastructure Security and Resilience*, and E.O. 13636, *Improving Critical Infrastructure Cybersecurity*. Both were issued to underscore the Federal Government's responsibility to strengthen the security and resilience of its own critical infrastructure, for the continuity of national essential functions, and to organize itself to partner effectively with and add value to the security and resilience efforts of critical infrastructure owners and operators.

This guide is designed to provide Federal employees, their supervisors, and agency security personnel with a framework for understanding and mitigating risks posed to an organization when instituting a mobile workplace. There are a wide range of potential threats that can be introduced to a government facility by telework/mobility. This document will address the security concerns associated with both government-furnished equipment (GFE) and personally owned equipment.

The authority for Federal departments and agencies to provide security for their facilities and employees is cited in various sections of the United States Code (USC) and the Code of Federal Regulations (CFR). It is beyond the scope of this document to cite individual department and agency authority. For more information regarding authorities, the reader should contact their agency Office of General Counsel (OGC). In accordance with their respective authority, each department or agency obtains the funds to provide security.

3.0   Introduction

Modern advances in technology now make it possible for an enterprise to continue operating under all but the most catastrophic circumstances. The workplace can be truly mobile, and it offers tremendous opportunities for the Federal Government. Many employees are no longer tied to a desk, let alone a single location, to complete the core tasks of their mission. A single flood or snowstorm no longer means agencies and departments grind to a halt for want of available employees. In light of this, Federal entities need to take full advantage of teleworking benefits when available.

Continuity of operations efforts can be augmented by teleworking capabilities. While this expands the operational boundaries, the use of teleworking must be conducted in accordance with Telework Enhancement Act of 2010. The nature of the agency's mission and certain functions may dictate activities be performed at dedicated continuity facilities with access to systems conforming to the National Communications Systems Directive 3-10.

The purpose of this document refers to the usage of information technologies (such as telecommunications and computers) for work-related activities. It moves the workplace to the workers, instead of moving the workers to the workplace that is the typical scenario for professionals.[2] In the Federal Government, the terms "telecommuting" and "telework" are used interchangeably, but telework is the official term and is defined in the Telework Enhancement Act as follows: "the term 'telework' or 'teleworking' refers to a work flexibility arrangement under which an employee performs the duties and responsibilities of such employee's position, and other authorized activities, from an approved worksite other than the location from which the employee would otherwise work."[3]

In practice, "telework" is a work arrangement allowing an employee to perform work during any part of regular paid hours at an approved alternative worksite (e.g., home, telework center). This definition of telework includes what is generally referred to as remote work but does not include any part of work done while on official travel or mobile work.[4] Even though outside of the official Federal definition, many agencies use the term telework to describe a wide range of work settings and alternative work practices better termed "mobile work" or "mobility." These could include, for example, working inside the office in areas other than assigned workstations, at home, outside the office while traveling, or in the field. Mobile work refers to an employee's ability to work freely inside and outside the office. Mobility also encompasses all remote work functionally required for a job. Telework is a sub-set of mobility wherein an employee works specifically at home or at a satellite office location near the employee's home. These guidelines include all forms of mobility as well as telework, and they are both used interchangeably.

---

[2] Refer to http://www.uscg.mil/hq/cg1/cg121/benefits/telework.asp.

[3] Public Law No. 111-292 of December 9, 2010 (The Telework Enhancement Act of 2010).

[4] OPM "Guide to Telework in the Federal Government: https://www.telework.gov/guidance-legislation/telework-guidance/telework-guide/.

4.0   Roles and Responsibilities

First Line Supervisors are responsible and accountable for supervising work in accordance with the Fair Labor Standards Act (FLSA).[5] All employees, teleworking or not, are required to follow established office practices, agency policies, and laws for requesting and obtaining approval of leave, overtime, or any change to the work schedule.

4.1   Terms of Telework Participation

Telework is a voluntary agreement between the employee and her or his supervisor. Employees are not required to telework, and supervisors are not required to offer the option if it presents hardships or security issues to the organization. Some agencies and divisions may have operational concerns negating the telework option (e.g., emergency operations centers, classified material handling).

However, in agencies or departments where telework is generally allowed, employees are required to complete a telework agreement and agency specific training[6] for use either on a routine basis or in emergency situations. This will allow the agency greater flexibility in circumstances, such as emergent weather conditions posing a risk to employee travel, where daily work can be completed at an alternative worksite. This will be especially true for those agencies and departments that must perform essential work regardless of conditions. In some cases, it may be the only viable means for a division to continue functioning.

4.2   Telework Eligibility and Participation

In certain situations, based on the criteria set forth in the Telework Enhancement Act of 2010, positions or employees may be identified as ineligible for telework. Exceptions to teleworking eligibility can be defined in part as an employee in a position requiring on a daily basis, meaning every standard business day, including the following:

- Direct handling of secure materials determined to be inappropriate for telework by the agency. Secure materials are those materials (a) where there exists a written policy (at the government, agency, or organizational level) restricting the use/access outside of a specific government installation or area within a government installation and/or (b) where appropriate mitigating IT security measures do not exist. Secure materials may include Personally Identifiable Information (PII).

- On-site work effort activity that cannot be handled remotely or at an appropriate alternative worksite.

Employees may not be authorized or allowed to continue to telework if the performance of the employee does not comply with the terms of the written telework agreement between the supervisor and employee. The limitations on eligibility even in emergency or other unforeseen situations set forth above are not intended to constitute an exhaustive listing of all of the possible

---

[5] Refer to the U.S. Department of Labor website for more information: https://www.dol.gov/.

[6] Refer to the Office of Personnel Management website for more information: https://www.telework.gov/.

reasons for limiting or restricting telework. All agency job announcements should indicate whether the position is eligible for telework.

4.3 Telework Managing Officer

The Telework Managing Officer (TMO) is an established senior level position with direct access to the appropriate level of department or agency leadership and is responsible for:

- Telework advocacy;
- Policy development and implementation related to agency telework programs;
- Providing expertise and guidance to agency leadership, including the agency head and human resources department;
- Primary senior level agency point of contact for the Office of Personnel Management (OPM) on telework matters; and
- Resource for managers and employees on telework matters.[7]

4.4 Telework Coordinator

An employee who as part of his or her official duties serves as a point of contact providing advocacy, local telework implementation support, and data collection on implementation of this policy at a regional, service, or staff office level. Telework coordinators provide information to and receive support from the TMO.

4.5 Privacy Office Oversight

The Privacy Office in each agency works to protect the privacy of all individuals and to ensure compliance with the Privacy Act (PA) of 1974, as amended, and related statutes, regulations, and Office of Management and Budget (OMB) directives, whether it is in a physical office or in a teleworking/mobile environment.[8] With expertise in privacy laws, both domestic and international, this office should inform privacy policy development both within the agencies and in collaboration with the rest of the Federal Government. This office should evaluate agency programs, systems, and initiatives for potential privacy impacts and provide mitigation strategies to reduce the privacy impact. Findings suggest it should be the responsibility of senior leadership to ensure privacy protections are implemented throughout an agency.

The mission of the Privacy Office should be to protect all individuals by embedding and enforcing privacy protections and transparency in all agency activities. Key responsibilities of any Privacy Office should include:

- Evaluating agency legislative and regulatory proposals involving the collection, use, and disclosure of PII;

---

[7] Refer to the Public Law 111-292: 5 USC § 6505: Telework Managing Officer: https://www.gsa.gov/graphics/ogp/PLAW111pub292.pdf.

[8] Refer to the Department of Justice web site regarding the Privacy Act of 1974 (5 USC § 552a): https://www.justice.gov/opcl/privacy-act-1974.

- Centralizing Freedom of Information Act (FOIA) and Privacy Act operations to provide policy and programmatic oversight, and support implementation across an agency;

- Operating an agency-wide Privacy Incident Response Program to ensure incidents involving PII are properly reported, investigated, and mitigated, as appropriate; and

- Responding to complaints of privacy violations and provide redress, as appropriate.

4.6 Telework Supervisor

Supervisors are responsible for establishing a telework agreement with eligible staff that meet the objectives of the office and the employee. Employees should familiarize themselves with their agency policy and any relevant procedures and collective bargaining agreements to ensure that they are in compliance with their requirements. Furthermore, supervisors will be responsible and accountable, pursuant to the Telework Enhancement Act of 2010, for treating all teleworking and non-teleworking employees the same in acts involving managerial discretion, including but not limited to:

- Distribution of assignments among all employees in the work unit, whether working at the agency worksite or at appropriate alternative worksites;

- Use of appropriate work tracking and communication tools regardless of whether they telework;

- Appropriate formal and informal feedback, which are essential for all employees to work effectively. Performance expectations set the level of individual performance that must be met for an employee's performance to be appraised at a particular level of success. All employees (teleworkers and non-teleworkers) should be evaluated consistent with the performance expectations in their performance plans;

- Adhere to agency sensitive and PII policy; and

- Other issues involving managerial discretion, including training, reassignment, promotions, reduction in grade, retention, and removal of employees.

Telework agreements remain in effect as stipulated by agency policy and any relevant procedures and collective bargaining agreements to ensure that they are in compliance with their requirements but can be modified in response to a supervisor's or employee's request, changes in position eligibility or employee eligibility, or to address the impact of telework on individual or organizational performance. All telework agreements and modifications of the agreement require mutual assent of the employee's supervisor and the employee.

The telework agreement shall include the designation of regular (routine), intermittent, or emergency telework that may be modified by mutual agreement between the employee and the supervisor. The supervisor and staff members participating in the telework program should periodically evaluate the telework agreement to determine if telework is meeting the objectives of the office and the member, and if modifications are needed. At a minimum, this evaluation should be done annually during the job performance review period. When there is a new supervisory/staff relationship, the telework agreement shall be re-signed or a new agreement executed.

4.7 Employee / Teleworker

Each department, agency, or organization should establish specific responsibilities for teleworking or mobility.[9] Suggested employee responsibilities include:

- Employees are in an official duty status while teleworking. Failure to adhere to applicable policies may result in, among other consequences, the imposition of specific limitations on telework, the termination of a telework agreement, and/or other penalties as outlined by the agency.

- It is the employee's responsibility to ensure the appropriate alternative worksite provides the work environment, connectivity, technology, resource access, and security consistent with the work effort. Supervisors retain the authority to overrule an employee's selection of a particular appropriate alternative worksite location if, in the supervisor's opinion, the location is not appropriate for business and/or fails to provide a working environment compliant with the conditions outlined in this policy.

- Employees are responsible for maintaining flexibility and responsiveness to the needs of the supervisor, employing organization, and work team. As with all work, employees are accountable for required individual contributions to team effort, and must communicate and collaborate appropriately; telework must support the efforts of the team and must not result in diminished individual, group/team, or organizational performance.

- Employees may be required to report to the agency worksite or other required location, pursuant to legitimate agency needs, for all or part of the workday during which they would otherwise telework. Cases of cancelled or interrupted plans to telework require appropriate advance notice to the employee, as outlined in the telework agreement. Except as otherwise provided in this policy, such cases do not (a) constitute a termination of the telework arrangement or (b) entitle the employee to a "replacement" or "in lieu of" telework day.

- Employees or timekeepers are responsible for documenting their telework in accordance with established processes, including agency-determined codes and tracking/reporting processes (e.g., completion and submission of time sheets or entering telework codes in their agency's electronic time and attendance system).

---

[9] Refer to the Office of Personnel Management website for more information on Telework 101 for Employees: https://www.telework.gov/training-resources/.

5.0 Security Considerations for Teleworking

As stated in *The Guide to Telework in the Federal Government*: "Federal agencies and staff are responsible for the security of Federal Government property, information, and information systems. Telework does not change this responsibility. If not properly implemented, telework may introduce vulnerabilities into agency systems and networks. To prevent security incidents, the Federal Information Security Management Act (FISMA) of 2002 requires agencies to protect information and information systems commensurate with risk. In addition, OMB memorandum M-06-16 and the Federal Information Processing Standard (FIPS) 140-2 encryption module recommend actions to protect remote information that all agencies should continue to implement. Agencies should refer to the National Institute of Science and Technology (NIST) security telework site for more information at http://csrc.nist.gov/telework/publications/index.html."[10]

The following is a list of considerations for secure teleworking:

- Use only authorized mechanisms, such as agency-provided virtual private network (VPN), Citrix, or other authorized remote access applications;

- Keep operating system and antivirus software up-to-date and maintain personal firewalls on devices used to access your agency network; and

- For physical security considerations refer to Section 7: Securing Equipment & Sensitive Materials for Teleworking and Alternative Environments.

The following is a general summary of good security practices on either agency provided or personal IT devices:

- Use strong passwords. Choose passwords that are difficult or impossible to guess. Maintain different passwords for all accounts. NIST provides excellent guidance on password creation and maintenance;[11] and

- Make regular backups of critical data according to agency policies.

Refer to agency policies for more information on cyber security measures.

5.1 Virtual Security

Alternative worksites, telework centers, and other remote locations are relied upon more and more by Federal enterprises for continuity of operations, extension of the normal work day, part-time and full-time teleworkers, and mobile work. This may enable Federal employees to connect to networks from remote locations on specified days or during emergencies, providing flexibility to support the mission. In order for the Federal telework staff to be optimally productive, they require access to the same services used at the physical Federal facilities, including data, e-mail, collaboration tools, and voice and video services in some instances.

Devices and processes enabling the extension of the physical workplace increased the risk of

---

[10] Refer to "Guide to Telework in the Federal Government," Office of Personnel Management, https://www.telework.gov/guidance-legislation/telework-guidance/telework-guide/.

[11] Refer to Special Publication 800-118 "Guide to Enterprise Password Management," http://csrc.nist.gov/publications/drafts/800-118/draft-sp800-118.pdf.

theft and unauthorized disclosure of data. The benefits of teleworking make it imperative to employ additional measures to protect these resources, including laptops and other mobile computing devices and the data they store and process.

OMB and the FIPS recommend all departments and agencies encrypt all data on mobile computers/devices that carry agency data unless the data is determined to be non-sensitive in writing or by an authorized official. A number of laws and regulations compel organizations to ensure sensitive information is appropriately protected. The following is a list of key regulations, standards, and guidelines:

- Federal Information Security Management Act of 2002;
- Privacy Act of 1974, as amended;
- Gramm-Leach-Bliley Act (GLBA); and
- Health Insurance Portability and Accountability Act (HIPAA) of 1996.

6.0 Security Considerations for Teleworking and Alternative Workplace Environments

Observations suggest it is important for agencies to consider the security risks in different telework environments when creating a telework policy. Each location available to employees needs to be carefully assessed as being an appropriate alternative worksite. Rules or procedures generally considered not necessary in one locale (office) may be necessary in another (e.g., encryption).

An appropriate alternative worksite is a location other than the agency worksite to which an employee is assigned (also called their duty station). It may include an employee's residence or other work location that supports productive work and provides the space, connectivity, and security appropriate to the work effort. These other locations may include telework centers, customer space, hotel rooms, and public spaces such as libraries, coffee shops, airport lounges, internet cafes, etc.

Each employee is responsible for ensuring they have an appropriate alternative worksite that provides the work environment, connectivity, technology, resources, and security necessary to accomplish their job. The employee must consider whether:

- Telework allows the appropriate level of interaction with the entire work group or team;

- The desired location choice will allow for a productive and secure work environment;

- The work to be accomplished can be completed effectively from the appropriate alternative worksite;

- The necessary tools and communication connections are available. For example, consider laptop connectivity and the wide range of local providers supporting internet access as some may not have the most reliable high speed connection and this could impact work production;

- There are distractions that could get in the way of productive telework. A coffee shop could be an appropriate alternative site, but with the general public coming in and out, there are obvious distractions if the job entails communicating with customers on the phone or participating in a conference call;

- The telework site provides appropriate security for the work as described in following sections; and

- Mobile devices should be properly secured according to agency policies.

6.1 Teleworking from Home

Federal agencies and staff are responsible for the security of Federal Government property, information, and information systems. Telework does not change this responsibility. If not properly implemented, telework may introduce vulnerabilities into agency systems and networks.

6.1.1 Potential Threats/Risks when Teleworking from Home

Teleworking from home raises other concerns for teleworkers, whether they are using their own computers or using government-furnished computers. Each agency should establish policies on types of equipment to use (e.g., GFE, personal computers) while teleworking and to ensure the adequacy of information and security protections for information and information systems used while teleworking.

If GFE is provided, it must be defined in agency policies that family members and friends of teleworkers are not authorized to use any GFE. If the agency policy allows teleworkers to use personal equipment, care must be taken to not allow others to access government files and information or inadvertently corrupt files and the agency's information system.

Refer to agency guidelines for more information.

6.1.2 Recommendations to Address Physical Threats when Teleworking from Home

Appropriate physical security of teleworking sites is necessary to reduce or eliminate the likelihood of the loss of work related information or equipment. Teleworkers are responsible for the security of all official data and protection of any GFE and property when teleworking.

A dynamic threat environment demands our utmost vigilance and discipline, we must refine existing protective measures to prevent or substantially mitigate any threat. The following are considerations when teleworking from home:

Guard information about yourself - maintain a low profile:

- Destroy all envelopes or other items that show your name or other personal information;

- Instruct your family and associates not to provide strangers with information about you or your family;

- Be cautious about giving out information regarding family travel plans or security measures and procedures;

- Consider removing your name on your home/mailbox; and

- Avoid the use of your name on answering machines.

Enhance your home's security:

- Brief family members on your residential security and safety procedures;

- Ensure family members learn a duress word;

- Advise associates or family members of your destination and anticipated time of arrival;

- Use peephole viewers before you open the door;

- Do not open the door to anyone until you know who it is;

- Ensure sufficient illumination exists around your residence;

- Be alert to strangers who are on or near property for no apparent reason; and

- Refuse to meet with strangers outside your workplace.

Consider these physical security measures:

- Hiding a key outside to ensure family members can get in if they lose their keys is not a good security consideration;

- Home security can be improved with self-help measures such as changing locks, securing windows, and improving outdoor lighting;

- Make sure windows lock securely and put a dowel or rod in sliding door tracks to keep them from being forced open;

- Keep valuables out of sight;

- Do not hide spare keys outside;

- Use an alarm system;

- Put gravel outside windows; and

- Ensure sliding doors cannot be lifted out and lay a rod in the track.

Consider the local threat when selecting your home:

- Location in a low crime area;

- Access to emergency services;

- Security measures such as visitor control;

- Strong crime prevention measures; and

- Well-maintained neighborhoods with effective community organizations generally have lower crime rates. Even so, lax security can make your home a target for criminal break-in. [12]

6.2 Teleworking in Public Spaces

Teleworkers should be aware of the potential for cyber and physical risks and threats when working in public spaces such as airports, internet cafes, coffee shops, or libraries. Each agency should determine guidelines on teleworking from public spaces.

External or third-party network connections in public spaces will increase the cyber risks for telework devices and communications, such as a laptop using a wireless hotspot at a coffee shop. The physical risks and threats are also increased while using computer devices in public spaces. Additional information to provide a more secure teleworking environment in public

---

[12] CJCS Pocket Card 5260 Individual Protective Measures.

spaces can be found in NIST Special Publication 800-114, *User's Guide to Securing External Devices for Telework.*[13]

6.2.1 Recommendations to Address Cyber Threats when Teleworking in Public Spaces

When teleworking in public spaces (e.g., libraries, coffee shops), teleworkers should be aware no reasonable expectation of privacy exists. Vulnerabilities still exist that can be exploited even when using GFE with a VPN. Because VPNs carry sensitive information over an unsecure network and often allow full access to an internal government agency network, they are attractive targets to hackers.

The following tips should be considered when connecting from a public location or unsecured internet connection:

- Ensure devices are fully updated over trusted (i.e., agency, home) networks;
- Use a VPN or other secure access solution provided by the agency or organization;
- Activate the VPN session immediately after connecting to a third-party network;
- Use firewall and malware protection against intrusion;
- Consider the use of a screen privacy filter to ensure data is visible only to the user directly in front of the monitor; and
- Ensure files are backed-up regularly.

6.2.2 Recommendations to Address Physical Threats when Teleworking in Public Spaces

The potential for physical risks and threats in public spaces is also greater than in the home or office. Threats in public spaces include theft of identifications and passwords, theft of information from computer or device screens, and physical loss of hardware or paperwork. Some steps that should be taken to reduce the physical risk and threats of working in public spaces include, but are not limited to:

- Lock current sessions when not using the computer or device;
- Set screensavers to automatically activate when computer or device has been idle a short time;
- Do not leave paperwork exposed for others to read;
- Do not wear clothing with government agency symbols or logos;
- Maintain possession of computers or devices (do not leave them unattended);
- Do not include rank, title, or organization information on luggage tags;

---

[13] NIST Special Publication 800-114, "User's Guide to Securing External Devices for Telework and Remote Access," November 2007, http://csrc.nist.gov/publications/nistpubs/800-114/SP800-114.pdf.

- Consider background noise that may cause problems during phone calls or create an unprofessional impression to the other caller(s);

- Consider distractions that may be detrimental to accomplishing necessary tasks; and

- If using a mobile phone, video conferencing, or instant messaging, speak quietly and choose locations where your phone conversations will not be overheard.

Awareness to/from work (in transit security)

- Look for tampering; look under and around your automobile;

- At all times, keep your doors locked and windows rolled up;

- Alter routes and avoid choke points;

- Alternate parking places; and

- Plan safe locations along your route.

Reduce your risk when working at public sites

- Identify an exit route;

- Identify a location to meet, if separated;

- Watch for suspicious behavior in others; and

- Notice suspicious objects.

Official/unofficial travel security

- State Department Travel Warnings should be consulted before taking trips across the US-Mexico border;

- Prior to travel: Receive area of responsibility (AOR) specific threat briefing by security officer;

- Hotel selection considerations: select an inside hotel room (away from the street-side window), preferably on the 4th–10th floors; and

- If traveling overseas, know the location of the closest U.S. embassy and other safe locations where you can find refuge or assistance.

6.3 Working in Offices Using Alternative Workplace Strategies

Alternative workplace strategies are work arrangements wherein an employee may not have a dedicated or assigned workspace at the regular (agency) worksite, but instead uses one of the following arrangements when working at that location:

- Desk sharing: an arrangement in which two or more employees are assigned to share a single workspace and each employee has a designated day or time for use of the workspace.

- Hoteling: an arrangement where employees use non-dedicated, non-permanent workspaces assigned for use by reservation on an as-needed basis.

- Hot desking (also known as free address or touchdown workspace): is an arrangement in which employees use non-dedicated, non-permanent workspaces on an unreserved, first come, first served basis.

For more information on potential threats/risks when working with Alternative Workplace Strategies, please see Section 6.3.1 below.

6.3.1 Recommendations when Working with Alternative Workplace Strategies

Planning considerations for a secure alternative workplace are vital. It is important to know where employees, emergency exits, and sensitive equipment are located. In addition, it is important to have an emergency preparedness plan for effective, creative workplace strategies that can minimize the impact of any disruption and ensure business continuity. The following list offers some recommendations:

- Provide a reservation system for securing workspace with check-in and automatic cancelation for no-shows;

- Provide universal access to agency networks from any workspace;

- Provide security escort for visitors that are hot desking or working in a secure alternative workspace;

- Provide peripherals to support a laptop such as power, computer charger, and mouse;

- Provide instructions on installing printers, and mark all printers with appropriate information to identify during installation;

- Provide ways for locating other employees in the building;

- Revise emergency plans to account for more mobile workers, including multiple floor monitors and specific locations to regroup after a building evacuation;

- Provide access to assistance such as a help desks and concierges; and

- Develop a "user's manual" for shared resources, including instruction for the use of facilities and equipment, space use protocols defining expected behaviors, and points of contact for questions or reporting problems. This can be an electronic document and should be informed by user feedback and agency best practices.

Refer to agency security organization for foreign based telework.

7.0 Securing Equipment & Sensitive Materials for Teleworking and Alternative Workplace Environments

Teleworking employees should secure all equipment and sensitive material while not in their office. They should also be familiar with, understand, and comply with their agency's information security policies and participate in agency information security training. Depending on the sensitivity of the information being handled, the home office may need to include security measures, such as locked file cabinets, similar to what may be used in the worksite.

7.1 Safeguarding Sensitive Materials

- Unassigned workstations (e.g., hoteling, hot desking): Provide for personal and organizational storage needs independent of the workstation. Individual storage space must be lockable and sized to provide storage for a laptop, limited files, and personal effects. Organizational storage should be based on trends toward more electronic file storage and mandated records retention.

- Field office and satellite office storage: Per agency mandates, provide organizational storage. Provide day lockers for temporary storage of visiting staff.

- Domicile storage requirements: Per agency requirements, secure government property and files to avoid access by unauthorized personnel (i.e., residents or visitors).

- Hotel room storage requirements: Use hotel safes where available to secure government equipment and documents. Report any losses immediately to hotel security and your agency.

- Vehicle storage requirements: Do not leave unattended government property in plain view when parking in locations with public access. If laptops or other equipment or files must be left in the vehicle, secure in the trunk or other location where they are not visible from outside the vehicle.

- Traveling via airline or commercial means: Store laptops and sensitive documents at your seat. If this is not possible, use an overhead bin immediately adjacent to your seat. Do not put computers or sensitive documents in checked baggage.

- Other locations: Secure government equipment and documents to prevent access from unauthorized personnel.

- Personally identifiable information (PII):
  - An employee or contractor should not physically take PII from agency facilities or access remotely (i.e., from locations other than agency facilities) without written permission from the employee's supervisor, the data owner, and the authorizing officials. Approvals should be filed with the employee's supervisor. This applies to electronic media (e.g., laptops, mobile phones), paper, and any other media (e.g., CDs/DVDs) that may contain PII.

o PII should be stored on network drives and/or in application databases with proper access controls (i.e., user ID/password) and made available only to those individuals with a valid need to know.

o Log all computer-readable data extracts from databases holding PII and verify each extract, including PII, has been erased within 90 days or its use is still required.

o Maintain computer-readable data extracts that include PII in an official log including creator, date, type of information, and user.

o All incidents involving data breaches that could result in identity theft must be reported per OMB Memorandum M-07-16, "Safeguarding Against and Responding to the Breach of Personally Identifiable Information."

o Agency-managed computers that collect and store PII must adhere to all PII requirements.

o Ensure employees and contractors have the proper background investigation before accessing PII.

o Comply with privacy training requirements for employees and contractors (internal and external).

- Media protection:

o Sanitize all data from information system media, both digital and non-digital, before disposing or reusing in accordance with agency standards.

o Restrict access to information system media (e.g., disk drives, diskettes, internal and external hard drives, and portable devices), including backup media, removable media, and media containing sensitive information to authorized individuals.

o Physically control and securely store information system media within controlled areas.

o Protect digital media during transport outside of controlled areas using a certified FIPS 140-2 encryption module; non-digital media should be protected according to agency policy.

For more information on Secure Transmission Considerations, please refer to Appendix B.

7.2 Reporting a Breach or Loss

Safeguarding PII in the possession of the government and preventing its breach are essential to ensure the government retains the trust of the American public. This is a responsibility shared by officials accountable for administering operational and privacy and security programs, legal counsel, Agencies' Inspectors General and other law enforcement, and public and legislative affairs.[14]

---

[14] Federal Information Security Management Act of 2002 (FISMA) and the Privacy Act of 1974.

7.2.1 Procedures for Reporting Possible PII, Sensitive, and Government Proprietary Information Breach

- Develop an agency reporting policy that satisfies the Breach Notification Policy requirement stipulated in OMB Memorandum M-07-16, *Safeguarding Against and Responding to the Breach of Personally Identifiable Information.*

- Provide definitions for critical terms.

- Develop employee response requirements and instructions, including a contact phone number and email address.

- Develop a department/agency response team. At a minimum, the team should consist of the Program Manager (PM) of the program involved with the information breach, the Chief Information Officer (CIO), the Chief Privacy Officer or Senior Official for Privacy, a representative from the Communications Office, the Legislative Affairs Office, the General Counsel's Office, and a representative from the Management Office of Budget and Procurement. This should include team guidance and protocols.

- There should be no distinction between suspected and confirmed breaches when reporting.

- Create procedures to share common threats, vulnerabilities, and incident-related information with the appropriate organizations.

- Breaches must be reported immediately to all applicable agency security offices.

8.0 Training

An agency must provide an interactive telework training program to all employees eligible to participate in the agency's telework program. Employees are required to complete telework training as part of the telework agreement development and to undertake such refresher or modified training as may be specified by the TMO or Telework Coordinator. Agencies may offer or require additional training. The agency Telework Coordinator or TMO should have information about any training the agency may offer.

- It is vital that all teleworkers understand the risks of physical and cyber security threats while teleworking. IT security training may be required by an agency to keep both remote and in-office users aware of requirements and responsibilities.

- A security awareness, training, and education program should be established by the CIO to ensure all agency and contractor support staff involved in the management, design, development, operation, and use of IT systems are aware of their responsibilities for safeguarding agency systems and information.

- Agencies should require employees and contractors (internal and external) to provide verification that security awareness training and privacy training approved by the agency has been completed in accordance to agency policy.

- Agencies should require employees and contractors (internal and external), who have significant information security responsibilities as defined by OPM 5 CFR Part 930 and agency IT security training policy, to provide verification that specialized IT security training, as defined in the policy, has been completed.

- Agencies should implement a policy that when employees fail to comply with annual awareness and specialized IT security training requirements it may result in termination of email privileges and authorizing officials can terminate system accounts.

- All agency employees and contractors who work with PII and/or sensitive information should complete agency privacy awareness training.

Refer to www.telework.gov for non-agency specific training. Refer to Appendix D: Training Scenario Example.

9.0 Health and Safety

The ISC encourages a proactive approach by teleworkers to ensure safe appropriate alternative worksites as well as safe work habits.

Teleworking staff should also maintain a safe work area adequate for the performance of official duties. Staff should complete a safety checklist self-certifying the space is safe and free from hazards. Each agency is encouraged to develop an appropriate safety checklist. Appendix C includes an example that can be used to develop an agency checklist. The example does not encompass every situation that may be encountered. Employees are encouraged to obtain, at their own cost, professional assistance with issues concerning appropriate electrical service or circuit capacity for residential worksites.

While in the act of performing official duties at an appropriate alternative worksite, teleworkers may be covered by the:

- Military Personnel and Civilian Employees Claims Act of 1964, as amended (31 U.S.C. 3721);

- Federal Tort Claims Act (FTCA), 28 U.S.C. 2671-2680;

- Federal Employees' Compensation Act (FECA), 5 U.S.C. Chapter 81;

- Occupational Safety & Health Act (OSHA) of 1970 (Public Law 91-596, December 29, 1970 with amendments through January 1, 2004); and

- Americans with Disabilities Act (ADA).

For more information on a safe teleworking environment, please refer to Appendix C: Example Employee Safety Template for Telework Program.

10.0 Continuity Planning

Continuity planning efforts can be augmented by teleworking capabilities. While this expands the operational boundaries, the use of teleworking must be conducted in accordance with the Telework Enhancement Act of 2010. Telework planning should include a firm understanding of department or agency continuity planning requirements. Continuity planning could supersede an agency's mobility and telework policy.

Federal Continuity Directives (FCDs) 1 and 2 provide direction to the Federal Executive Branch for developing continuity plans and programs. Continuity planning facilitates the performance of executive branch essential functions during all-hazards emergencies or other situations that may disrupt normal operations.

FCD 1 defines continuity as the uninterrupted ability to provide services and support, while maintaining organizational viability, before, during, and after an event or incident. Continuity planning, including work arrangements such as telework and mobile work concepts, enhance the resiliency and continuity capability of organizations.[15] It further states that Continuity of Operations (COOP) is an effort within individual organizations to ensure they can continue to perform their essential functions during a wide range of emergencies including localized acts of nature, accidents, and technological or attack related emergencies.

Continuity planning is good business practice to ensure the execution of a department's or agency's operating functions through all circumstances. Today's threat environment and the potential for no-notice emergencies, including acts of nature, accidents, critical cyber and communication infrastructure emergencies, and military or terrorist attack-related incidents, increase the need for robust continuity capabilities and planning.

Modern advances in technology now make it possible for an enterprise to take advantage of capabilities that allow continued operations under most circumstances. Federal entities need to utilize the benefits of teleworking and mobile workplace in their continuity planning. Employees are not always tied to their desks or a single location to complete their mission essential functions. A single flood or snowstorm does not have to mean agencies and departments grind to a halt for want of available employees.

The nature of the agency's mission and certain functions may dictate activities be performed at dedicated continuity facilities with access to systems conforming to the National Communications Systems Directive 3-10. Furthermore, the nature of a continuity event may preclude the ability to use telework (e.g., communications capabilities may be severely degraded or staff may be incapacitated).

For more information on Continuity Planning, please refer to Appendix E: Individual Preparedness Continuity.

---

[15] Federal Continuity Directive 1, Federal Executive Branch National Continuity Program and Requirements, October 2012.

11.0 References

- Americans with Disabilities Act

- The Telework Enhancement Act of 2010 - Public Law No. 111-292 of December 9, 2010 requires the head of each executive agency to establish and implement a policy under which employees may be authorized to telework. This law does not establish telework as a right, nor does it make it mandatory.

- OMB Memorandum 07-16, Safeguarding Against and Responding to the Breach of Personally Identifiable Information, dated May 22, 2007

- OPM Telework 101 for Employees

- U.S. Office of Personnel Management, Federal Investigative Services: POLICY ON THE PROTECTION OF PERSONALLY IDENTIFIABLE INFORMATION (PII), August 2012

- "Guide to Enterprise Telework and Remote Access Security," National Institute of Science and Technology (NIST) Special Publication 800-46, rev. 1

- "Guide to Enterprise Password Management," National Institute of Science and Technology (NIST) Special Publication 800-118, (Draft)

- "Electronic Authentication Guideline," National Institute of Science and Technology (NIST) Special Publication 800-63-1

- General Services Administration (GSA) Presentation Slides on Suite 7300 - Piloting Workspace

- E.O. 12977

- E.O. 13286

- Department of Energy Office of Health, Safety, and Security "Desk Reference on Telework Program," December 2011

- DoD 5200.1-R, "Information Security Program," January 14, 1997

- GSA Order, GSA Mobility and Telework Policy, Update HCO 6040.1

- GSA definition and as set forth in 300 FTR 300-3.1

- OPM definition and as set forth in 5 CFR 531.605

- Public Law No. 106-346 of October 23, 2000

- Fair Labor Standards Act (FLSA) - a federal law that establishes minimum wage, overtime pay, recordkeeping, and youth employment standards affecting employees in the private sector and in Federal, state, and local governments. In addition, the FLSA exempts specified employees or groups of employees from the application of certain of its provisions. As such, every employee is categorized, based on his or her job, as either exempt or nonexempt. The FLSA is published in sections 201-219 of title 29, United States Code (U.S.C.). Additional guidance may be found in the GSA Time and Leave

Administration Handbook, OAD P 6010.4, Chapters 11 and 12. OPM has more information at http://www.opm.gov/flsa.

- Military Personnel and Civilian Employees Claims Act of 1964, as amended (31 U.S.C. 3721)

- Federal Tort Claims Act (28 U.S.C. 2671-2680)

- Federal Employees' Compensation Act (FECA) (5 U.S.C. Chapter 81)

- Office of Personnel Management (OPM) Guide to Telework in the Federal Government, April 2011

- Personally identifiable information (PII) - as specified in OMB M-06-19

- Presidential Policy Directive (PPD-21), Critical Infrastructure Security and Resilience 2.12.2013

- Executive Order 13636: Improving Critical Infrastructure Cybersecurity

- National Communications Systems Directive 3-10

- Federal laws, regulations, and GSA policies:

  o Federal Information Security Management Act (FISMA) of 2002

  o Clinger-Cohen Act of 1996 also known as the "Information Technology Management Reform Act of 1996"

  o Federal Financial Management Improvement Act of 1996 (FFMIA); OMB Implementation Guidance for the FFMIA

  o Paperwork Reduction Act (PRA) of 1995 (Public Law 104-13)

  o Federal Managers Financial Integrity Act (FMFIA) (Public Law 97-255)

  o Government Paperwork Elimination Act (GPEA) (Public Law 105-277)

  o Privacy Act of 1974 (5 U.S.C. § 552a)

  o Homeland Security Presidential Directive (HSPD-20), "National Continuity Policy"

  o Homeland Security Presidential Directive (HSPD-12), "Policy for a Common Identification Standard for Federal Employees and Contractors"

  o Homeland Security Presidential Directive (HSPD-7), "Critical Infrastructure Identification, Prioritization, and Protection"

  o Office of Management and Budget (OMB) Circular A-130, "Management of Federal Information Resources," and Appendix III, "Security of Federal Automated Information Systems as amended"

  o DHS S&T Telework Policy

  o GSA Order 9297.2B, "GSA Information Breach Notification Policy"

  o GSA Order CIO 2110.2, "GSA Enterprise Architecture Policy"

- o GSA Order CIO 2135.2B, "GSA Information Technology (IT) Capital Planning and Investment Control"
- o GSA Order CIO P 2181.1, "GSA HSPD-12 Personal Identity Verification and Credentialing Handbook"
- o GSA Order ADM 7800.11A, "Personal Use of Agency Office Equipment"
- o GSA Order 2100.2A, "GSA Wireless LAN Security"
- o GSA Order CIO P 2140.3, "Systems Development Life Cycle (SDLC) Policy"
- o GSA Order CIO P 2165.1, "GSA Internal Telecommunications Management"
- o GSA Order CIO 2160.2B, "GSA Electronic Messaging and Related Services"
- o GSA Order CIO 2104.1, "GSA Information Technology (IT) General Rules of Behavior"
- o GSA Order CPO 1878.1, "GSA Privacy Act Program"
- o GSA Order ADM P 9732.1D, "Suitability and Personnel Security"
- o GSA Order CIO P 2182.1, "Mandatory Use of Personal Identity Verification (PIV) Credentials"
- o NIST: Security Issues for Telecommuting
- o "The Information Infrastructure: Reaching Society's Goals," NIST Special Publication 868

12.0 Interagency Security Committee Participants

<u>ISC Chair</u>
Caitlin Durkovich
Assistant Secretary for Infrastructure Protection
U.S. Department of Homeland Security

<u>Program Director</u>
Daryle Hernandez
Interagency Security Committee

<u>Operations Director</u>
Bernard Holt
Interagency Security Committee

<u>ISC Working Group Chair</u>
Sue Armstrong
Federal Protective Service

<u>Working Group Members</u>

Joseph Carriuolo
Federal Protective Service

Trent DePersia
DHS/Science and Technology

Megan K. Drohan
Interagency Security Committee

Veronica Givens
Office of Personnel Management

Bernard Holt
Interagency Security Committee

Charles King
Federal Trade Commission

Brett Knutson
United States Marshal Service

Michael Mulligan
DHS/Cybersecurity & Communications

Rob Obenreder
General Services Administration

Jimmy Ogletree
United States Marshal Service

Ashley Pearce
Federal Protective Service

Geralyn Praskievicz
Department of Energy

Antonio Reynolds, Sr.
Interagency Security Committee

Jerry Stanphill
Federal Aviation Administration

List of Abbreviations/Acronyms/Initializations

ADA	Americans with Disabilities Act
AOR	Area of Responsibility
AWA	Alternative Workplace Arrangement
CFR	Code of Federal Regulations
CIO	Chief Information Officer
COOP	Continuity of Operations
CUI	Controlled Unclassified Information
DHS	Department of Homeland Security
EO	Executive Order
FCD	Federal Continuity Directive
FECA	Federal Employees' Compensation Act
FIPS	Federal Information Processing Standard
FISMA	Federal Information Security Management Act
FLSA	Fair Labor Standards Act
FOIA	Freedom of Information Act
FTCA	Federal Tort Claims Act
GFE	Government-Furnished Equipment
GLBA	Gramm-Leach-Bliley Act
GSA	General Services Administration
HIPPA	Health Insurance Portability and Accountability Act
HRO	Human Resource Office
ISC	Interagency Security Committee
IT	Information Technology
NIST	National Institute of Science and Technology
OGC	Office of General Counsel
OMB	Office of Management and Budget
OPM	Office of Personnel Management
OSHA	Occupational Safety & Health Act
PA	Privacy Act
PII	Personally Identifiable Information
PM	Program Manager
PPD-21	Presidential Policy Directive 21
TMO	Telework Managing Officer
U.S.C.	United States Code
VPN	Virtual Private Network

Glossary of Terms

TERM	DEFINITION
Agency Worksite	The regular worksite for the employee's position of record; the physical address or place where the employee would work if not teleworking.
Alternative Workplace Arrangement	A work arrangement in which an employee has no dedicated/assigned workspace at the regular (agency) worksite, but instead uses hoteling, hot desking, or desk sharing when working at that location.
Appropriate Alternative Worksite	Worksite other than the agency worksite, including employee's residence or other work location that supports productive work and provides an environment, connectivity, and security appropriate to the work effort.
Client Device	A system used by a remote worker to access an organization's network and the systems on that network.
Client Site	A space that can be the used by a Federal employee at a contractor or support contractor's facility on an intermittent basis. It can also be defined as space that a contractor or support contractor uses at a Federal facility on a regular or intermittent basis.
Consumer Device	A small, usually mobile computer that does not run a standard PC OS or that runs a standard PC OS but does not permit users to access it directly. Examples of consumer devices are networking-capable personal digital assistants (PDA), cell phones/smart phones, and video game systems.
Controlled Unclassified Information	A categorical designation that identifies unclassified information throughout the executive branch that requires safeguarding or dissemination controls, pursuant to and consistent with applicable law, regulations, and government-wide policies.
Desk sharing	An alternative workplace arrangement in which two or more employees share use of a single workspace where each employee has a designated day or time for use of the workspace.
Direct Application Access	A high-level remote access architecture that allows teleworkers to access an individual application directly, without using remote access software.

TERM	DEFINITION
Hot Desking (also known as free address or touchdown workstations)	An alternative workplace arrangement in which employees use non-dedicated, non-permanent workspaces in the primary agency worksite on an unreserved first come, first served basis (typically drop-in).
Hoteling	An alternative workplace arrangement where employees use non-dedicated, non-permanent workspaces assigned for use by reservation on an as-needed basis.
Mobile Work (Mobility)	Mobile work (mobility) refers to an employee's ability to work freely inside and outside the office. Mobility also encompasses all remote work that is functionally required for a job. Telework is a sub-set of mobility in which an employee works specifically at home or at an approved alternative worksite such as a satellite office.
Official Travel	Travel under an official travel authorization from an employee's official station or other authorized point of departure to a temporary duty location and return from a temporary duty location, between two temporary duty locations, or relocation at the direction of a Federal agency.

TERM	DEFINITION
Official worksite/duty station	Pursuant to the OPM definition and as set forth in 5 CFR 531.605, official worksite is the location where the employee regularly performs his or her official work duties. Changes in an employee's official worksite may affect employee pay, locality pay and travel funding responsibilities and must be processed by the servicing Human Resources Office. Designation of the official worksite must be determined on a case-by-case basis using the following considerations: • The official worksite is the location of the agency worksite for the employee's position - the place where the employee would normally work if not teleworking - as long as the employee is scheduled to report physically at least twice each biweekly pay period to that agency worksite; • The official worksite for an employee who is not scheduled to report at least twice a biweekly pay period to the agency worksite (includes virtual workers/full time teleworkers) is the location of the appropriate alternative worksite (except in certain temporary duty situations); • The official worksite for an employee whose work location varies on a recurring basis (mobile work), and who does not report at least twice each biweekly pay period to the agency worksite, is the agency worksite, as long as the employee is performing work within the same geographic area (established for the purpose of a given pay entitlement) as the agency worksite.
Personally Identifiable Information	Any information that permits the identity of an individual to be directly or indirectly inferred, including information that is linked or linkable to an individual.
Personal Computer/Equipment	A desktop or laptop computer running a standard PC operating system (e.g., Windows Vista, Windows XP, Linux/Unix, and Mac OS X).
Portal	A high-level remote access architecture that is based on a server that offers teleworkers access to one or more applications through a single centralized interface.
Public Space	An area within a building to which there is free access by the public, such as a foyer or lobby.
Remote Access	The ability for an organization's users to access its non-public computing resources from external locations other than the organization's facilities.

TERM	DEFINITION
Remote Desktop Access	A high-level remote access architecture that gives a teleworker the ability to remotely control a particular desktop computer at the organization, most often the user's own computer at the organization's office, from a telework client device.
Session Locking	A feature that permits a user to lock a session upon demand or locks the session after it has been idle for a preset period of time.
Social Engineering	An attempt to trick someone into revealing information (e.g., a password) that can be used to attack systems or networks. (ref. NIST 800-63-1)
Telecommuting	See "Telework."
Telework	The official definition of "telework" can be found in the Telework Enhancement Act of 2010: "[t]he term 'telework' or 'teleworking' refers to a work flexibility arrangement under which an employee performs the duties and responsibilities of such employee's position, and other authorized activities, from an approved worksite other than the location from which the employee would otherwise work."
Telework Client Device	A PC or consumer device used by a teleworker for performing telework.
Telework Agreement	A formal written agreement between a supervisor and an employee to permit the employee to telework as defined within agency policy.
Telework Policy	A policy under which eligible employees of the agency may participate in telecommuting to the maximum extent possible without diminished employee performance.
Satellite Office	A small office in a different location from a company or government agency's main office.
Unscheduled Telework	A form of telework that allows employees to telework without previous supervisory approval in response to specific announcements by OPM or other local government deciding/authorizing officials regarding emergency situations. It is a means for agency employees to continue work operations and maintain productivity during emergency situations.
Virtual Private Network	A virtual network, built on top of existing physical networks, that provides a secure communications tunnel for data and other information transmitted between networks.

TERM	DEFINITION
Virtual officing worksite/distributed work environment	An alternative workplace arrangement in which a work group, team, or organization has no permanent physical worksite (building or other physical location) to which the employees report for meetings or other work related matters. Instead, the work setting is characterized by employees using a communications medium such as computer network access and/or other communications applications that enhance collaborative work and/or other interpersonal business interactions. The physical locations of employees working in a virtual office or distributed work environment may be any appropriate alternative worksite.
Virtual Worker/Employee	A full time teleworker whose official worksite (duty station) is an appropriate alternative worksite. The appropriate alternative worksite may be inside or outside the local commuting area of the agency worksite and include such places as the employee's residence.
Working/Business Hours	To be specified by the agency telework agreement.

Appendix A: Recommendations to Address Cyber Threats when Teleworking from Home

A.1 Wired Network

Ensure your network is protected from threats from the internet. This is easily done by purchasing a router or switch with a built-in firewall. The router connects directly to a cable or DSL modem on one interface and allows many computers to plug into the other interface.

Personal software firewalls and anti-virus software installed on a workstation may provide additional endpoint protection from malware when browsing the internet, and these security controls should be required to access resources on the agency network.

Do not install personal firewall software on an agency-furnished computer. Remember to change the router's default administrative password and, if possible, disable any management interfaces that can be accessed remotely from an external IP address (e.g., a web management interface that can be accessed from outside your residence).

A.2 Wireless Network

For a wireless network, protection is needed from internet-based threats while securing the network against local threats to the wireless network. High-powered antennas have been successfully used to access wireless networks at great distances, meaning a personal network is accessible by neighbors and war-drivers (hackers that drive around trying to find insecure wireless networks) up to several blocks away. Many of the same wired security principles can be applied to wireless networking. Ensuring that the purchased wireless access points also include a router/switch/firewall is critical. If not, purchase the same type as defined in the wired paragraph above.

As previously indicated, remember to change the router's default administrative password and disable any management interfaces that can be accessed remotely from an external IP address.

Once secured from the internet threats, secure the wireless portion of your network. Implement the following settings on the wireless access point and computers:

- Enable Wi-Fi Protected Access 2 (WPA2) on the wireless connection. WPA2 replaced WPA and WEP and is based on much stronger security protocols.

- Pick a strong passphrase for WPA2; the Wi-Fi Alliance, a non-profit industry association of leading Wi-Fi companies, recommends a passcode length of at least 20 characters that combines letters, numbers and symbols, with no discernible words.

This will not make the network impenetrable, but it will go a long way in reducing the risk of compromise. The user manual that came with the wireless access point should provide additional guidance for enabling these settings.

Additional security settings and enhancements that are outside the scope of this document can be found on the website of the Wi-Fi Alliance at http://www.wi-fi.org/.

Appendix B: Secure Transmission Considerations

Telework requires special precautions when handling agency information, especially sensitive or FOUO information. Classified information should never be transmitted through unauthorized or unsecured channels.

B.1 Transmission of PII and Sensitive Material

- All sensitive information, such as PII, transmitted outside the agency firewall must be encrypted. Certified encryption modules must be used in accordance with Federal Information Processing Standards (FIPS) Publication 140-2, "Security requirements for Cryptographic Modules."

- For non-electronic transmittal of PII, limit access of PII only to those individuals authorized to handle it, create a paper trail, and verify information reached its destination.

- When sending PII by courier, mark "signature required" when sending documents. This creates a chain of custody in the event items are misplaced or lost.

- When printing documents containing PII, do not let documents sit on a printer where unauthorized personnel may have access to the information.

- When faxing information use a secure fax line. If one is not available, contact the recipient prior to faxing, so they know information is coming. Contact the recipient after transmission to ensure they received it.

- Portable Device Storage of PII:

  o If it is a business requirement to store PII on agency user workstations or mobile devices such as notebook computers, CD-ROMs/DVDs, personal digital assistants, authorized USB drives, and mobile phones, PII should be encrypted using a FIPS 140-2 certified encryption module.

B.2 Encryption

- Encrypt all stored passwords.

- All sensitive information, such as PII, transmitted outside the agency firewall should be encrypted. Certified encryption modules must be used in accordance with FIPS PUB 140-2, "Security requirements for Cryptographic Modules."

- When using password generated encryption keys, a password of at least 8 characters with a combination of letters, numbers, and special characters should be required. A password of at least 12 characters is recommended.

Appendix C: Example Employee Safety Template for Telework Program

The following example is designed to assess the overall safety of the alternative worksite if it is in a non-government owned or leased site (i.e., a residence). The participating employee should complete this self-certification checklist, sign, date, and return it to their agency telework coordinator. The employee should retain a copy for his or her records.

Participating Employee Name:			
Position Title:		Pay Plan-Series-Grade:	
Name of Organization:			
Supervisor's Name:			
Home Address:	City & State:	Zip Code:	
Home Telephone (include Area Code):	Work Telephone (include Area Code):	Cell Telephone (include Area Code):	
Describe the designated work area at the alternative worksite:			

List of items/conditions to inspect; Check Yes, No, or Not Applicable (N/A) as appropriate.			
Workplace Environment. This section is designed to ensure a safe workplace environment. A "No" response indicates that a safety and health issue may exist and a remedy/correction is required to participate in the agency telework program.			
A. Are temperatures, noise, ventilation, and lighting levels adequate for maintaining your normal level of job performance?	☐ Yes	☐ No	☐ N/A
B. Are all circuit breakers and/or fuses in the electrical panel labeled as to intended service?	☐ Yes	☐ No	☐ N/A
C. Do circuit breakers clearly indicate if they are in the open or closed position?	☐ Yes	☐ No	☐ N/A
D. Will the building's electrical system permit the grounding of electrical equipment (i.e., a three-prong receptacle)?	☐ Yes	☐ No	☐ N/A
E. Are all stairs with four (4) or more steps that are used to get to the work area equipped with handrails?	☐ Yes	☐ No	☐ N/A
F. Are aisles, doorways, and corners free of obstructions to permit visibility and movement?	☐ Yes	☐ No	☐ N/A
G. Are file cabinets and storage closets arranged so drawers and doors do not enter into walkways?	☐ Yes	☐ No	☐ N/A

List of items/conditions to inspect; Check Yes, No, or Not Applicable (N/A) as appropriate.			
Workplace Environment. This section is designed to ensure a safe workplace environment. A "No" response indicates that a safety and health issue may exist and a remedy/correction is required to participate in the agency telework program.			
H. Are phone lines, electrical cords, and surge protectors secured under a desk or alongside a baseboard?	☐ Yes	☐ No	☐ N/A
I. Is the floor surfaces dry, level, and adequately maintained?	☐ Yes	☐ No	☐ N/A
J. Are carpets well secured to the floor and free of frayed or worn seams?	☐ Yes	☐ No	☐ N/A
K. Is there a smoke detector in or near the work area?	☐ Yes	☐ No	☐ N/A
L. Do you have an emergency or contingency plan in place with emergency telephone numbers and means of escape?	☐ Yes	☐ No	☐ N/A
M. Is there enough light for reading?	☐ Yes	☐ No	☐ N/A
Computer Station (if applicable). This section is intended to help you create a safe and comfortable computer workstation in accordance with the Department of Labor, Occupational Safety and Health Administration guidance. A "No" response indicates that an ergonomic issue may exist and should be remedied/corrected prior to participating in the agency telework program.			
A. Is your chair adjustable?	☐ Yes	☐ No	☐ N/A
B. Are temperatures, noise, ventilation, and lighting levels adequate for maintaining your normal level of job performance?	☐ Yes	☐ No	☐ N/A
C. Is your back adequately supported by a backrest?	☐ Yes	☐ No	☐ N/A
D. Are all circuit breakers and/or fuses in the electrical panel labeled as to intended service?	☐ Yes	☐ No	☐ N/A
E. Do you know how to adjust your chair?	☐ Yes	☐ No	☐ N/A
F. Do circuit breakers clearly indicate if they are in the open or closed position?	☐ Yes	☐ No	☐ N/A
G. Are your feet on the floor or fully supported by a footrest?	☐ Yes	☐ No	☐ N/A
H. Are you satisfied with the placement of your computer monitor, mouse, and keyboard?	☐ Yes	☐ No	☐ N/A
I. Is it easy to read the text on your screen?	☐ Yes	☐ No	☐ N/A
J. Do you have enough leg room at your desk?	☐ Yes	☐ No	☐ N/A
K. Is the computer monitor screen free from noticeable glare?	☐ Yes	☐ No	☐ N/A
L. Is the top of the computer monitor screen at eye level?	☐ Yes	☐ No	☐ N/A
M. Is there space to rest your arms while not keying?	☐ Yes	☐ No	☐ N/A
N. When keying, are your forearms parallel with the floor?	☐ Yes	☐ No	☐ N/A
O. Are your wrists fairly straight when keying?	☐ Yes	☐ No	☐ N/A

Employee Certification	
I certify the above answers to be true and correct to the best of my knowledge and belief and are made in good faith.	
Employee Signature	Date
Supervisor Signature	Date
Telework Coordinator Signature	Date

Appendix D: Training Scenario Example

Completing Work at Home

An organization's employee needed to leave early for a doctor's appointment, but the employee was not finished with her work for the day and had no leave time available. Since she had the same spreadsheet application at home, she decided to email a data extract as an attachment to her personal email address and finish her work at home that evening. The data extract was downloaded from an access-controlled human resources database located on a server within the organization's security perimeter. This data extract contained employee names, identification numbers, birth dates, salary information, manager names, addresses, phone numbers, and positions.

When she arrived home that evening, she logged into her personal email address, downloaded the data extract to her family's computer, and used her spreadsheet application to analyze the data. The following are additional questions for this scenario:

- Which data elements contained in this data extract should be considered PII?

- What is the PII confidentiality impact level? What factors were taken into consideration when making this determination?

- What privacy-specific safeguards might help protect the PII contained in the data extract?

- How could the employer have prevented this situation?

- What should the employee do with the copies of the extract when she finishes her work?

- Should the emailing of the extract to a personal email address be considered a breach?

- What could the organization do to reduce the likelihood of similar events in the future?

- How should this scenario be handled if the information is a list of de-identified retirement income statistics? Would the previous questions be answered differently?

Appendix E: Individual Preparedness Continuity

The Department of Homeland Security's Federal Emergency Management Agency (FEMA) recommends keeping items included in Appendix E on hand in case of emergency. Please visit www.Ready.gov for more information regarding emergency personal preparedness.

It is recommended to have at least three days' worth of basic supplies on hand to survive when an emergency occurs. The checklist below contains some basic items every personal emergency go-kit should include.

It is important that individuals consider location and the unique family needs in order to create a customized emergency go-kit. Individuals should also consider having multiple emergency go-kits, one for home and smaller portable kits in their workplace, vehicle, or other places they frequent.

E.1 Basic Emergency Go Kit

- Water, one gallon per person per day for at least three days;
- Food, at least a three-day supply of non-perishable food;
- Manual or non-electric can opener for food (if necessary);
- Battery powered or hand crank radio with NOAA Weather capability and extra batteries;
- Rapid charger for mobile devices;
- Flashlight and extra batteries, glow or light sticks;
- First aid kit;
- Whistle to signal for help;
- Dust mask to help filter contaminated air;
- Toilet paper, baby wipes, garbage bags and plastic ties for personal sanitation;
- Wrench or pliers to turn off utilities;
- Local maps;
- Prescription medication, glasses and personal hygiene items;
- Important family documents in waterproof container; including emergency contact lists;
- Cash or travelers checks;
- Sleeping bags and warm blankets;
- Fire extinguishers; and
- Matches in waterproof container.

Store kit in an easily accessible location in the home and ensure everyone is aware of the location. If young children are present, ensure the kit includes toys, books, and other personal items for children.

E.2 Emergency Plan Card

An Emergency Plan Card can be used to collect vital information required to locate individuals and keep them connected. It also serves to remind everyone of the basic emergency plan in the event of an incident. The card can be used as a training device for younger individuals to help them stay focused during an emergency in the absence of adult supervision.

- Personal identification information;
- School information;
- Parent/guardian information;
- Emergency meeting locations;
- Important contact information;
- Alternative caretaker information;
- Conduct Familiarization Training with Family Members;
- Teach your children how to make telephone calls and how to dial 911 for emergency assistance;
- Program emergency numbers into all phones;
- Select predetermined locations where your family will reunite after an emergency;
- A location near your home;
- An alternate location in the event returning home after an emergency is not feasible;
- Ensure everyone knows the addresses and phone numbers of both meeting places;
- Know and practice all possible exit routes from your home and neighborhood;
- Get a copy of your child's school or daycare emergency plans;
- Make plans for where you can meet your child after an evacuation;
- Make sure that the school has up-to-date contact information for you and other family members; and
- Pre-authorize a friend or family member to pick up your child from school in case of emergency.

E.3 Office Go Kit

In the event an emergency occurs while at work, a personal go-kit at the office will enhances the ability to react and recover. This allows for self-sufficiency that diminishes the reliance on emergency responders and creates a focused response environment. Creating a personal go-kit for the office is beneficial for shelter-in-place emergencies, evacuations, and general personal care. See Figure 1 below.

Suggested Emergency Drive Away Kit Contents	

• Identification and charge (credit cards)
   ✓ Government identification card
   ✓ Driver's License
   ✓ Government travel card
   ✓ Health insurance card
   ✓ Personal charge (credit) card
• Communication equipment
   ✓   Pager / Blackberry
   ✓   Government cell phone
   ✓   Personal cell phone
   ✓   Government Emergency
         Telephone Service Card
• Hand-carried vital records
• Directions to continuity facility
• Business and leisure clothing
• Continuity plan
	• Business and personal contact numbers
	   ✓ Emergency phone numbers and addresses
	     (relatives, medical doctor, pharmacist, etc.)
	• Toiletries
	• Glow or light sticks, wind-up flashlight
	• Bottled water and non-perishable food (i.e.,
	  granola, dried fruit, energy bars, etc.)
	• Medical needs
	   ✓ Insurance information
	   ✓ List of allergies / blood type
	   ✓ Hearing aids and extra batteries
	   ✓ Glasses and contact lenses
	   ✓ Non-perishable prescription drugs (30-day
	     supply)
	   ✓ Over-the-counter medications, dietary
	     supplements

Figure 1: Suggested Emergency Drive Away Kit List

The stock in an emergency kit should be examined or rotated every ninety (90) days to ensure contents are fresh or have not spoiled. Batteries, most food stocks, and certain prescription medications have a shelf-life (i.e., expiration date). In the case of prescription medications, the efficacy of the drug diminishes over time and, in rare circumstances, can even become toxic once the expiration date is exceeded. Medications requiring refrigeration, like injectable insulin, cannot be stored in an emergency kit. These precautions should also be followed for over-the-counter medications.

Environmental and storage conditions of the kit should be considered as well. Emergency kits should be kept in a cool – not cold – and dry location. Kits should not be exposed to extreme temperature fluctuations (e.g., freeze-thaw cycles) as that can lead to spoilage of food stuffs and diminish the shelf-life of other items. Also, batteries exposed to cold conditions drain more rapidly. If possible, the kit should also be kept in a dark area if the container is transparent in any manner. Bottled water that is not distilled (e.g., heated before packaging) can grow algae if exposed to light. Some medications are also adversely affected by light exposer. Fluorescent lights, including long-tube and compact varieties, give off varying amounts of ultra-violet (UV) light and can adversely affect kit contents in the same way as exposure to direct sunlight, although it takes longer.